Knotting

Make your own basketball nets, guitar straps,
sports bags and more!

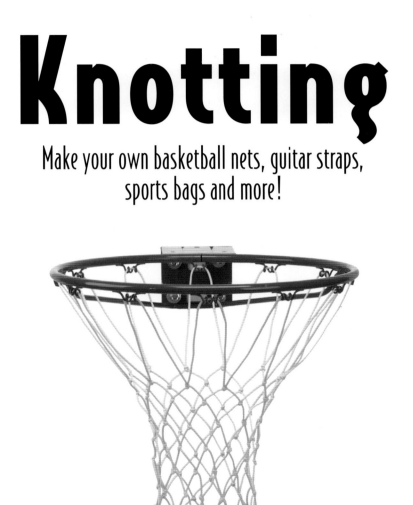

Written by Judy Ann Sadler
Illustrated by Céleste Gagnon

KIDS CAN PRESS

To Denby, who has always tied my heart in knots.

Text © 2006 Judy Ann Sadler
Illustrations © 2006 Kids Can Press

KIDS CAN DO IT and the ❧ logo are trademarks of Kids Can Press Ltd.

Kids Can Press acknowledges the financial support of the Government of Ontario,
through the Ontario Media Development Corporation's Ontario Book Initiative, and the
Government of Canada, through the BPIDP, for our publishing activity.

Published in Canada by
Kids Can Press Ltd.
29 Birch Avenue
Toronto, ON M4V 1E2

Published in the U.S. by
Kids Can Press Ltd.
2250 Military Road
Tonawanda, NY 14150

www.kidscanpress.com

Edited by Laurie Wark
Designed by Kathleen Collett
Illustrations by Céleste Gagnon
Cover photography by Ray Boudreau
Interior photography by Frank Baldassarra
Printed and bound in China

The hardcover edition of this book is smyth sewn casebound.
The paperback edition of this book is limp sewn with a drawn-on cover.

CM 06 0 9 8 7 6 5 4 3 2 1
CM PA 06 0 9 8 7 6 5 4 3 2 1

Library and Archives Canada Cataloguing in Publication

Sadler, Judy Ann, 1959–
Knotting : Make your own basketball nets, guitar straps, sports bags and more / written
by Judy Ann Sadler ; illustrated by Céleste Gagnon.

(Kids can do it)
Age level: 8–12.

ISBN-13: 978-1-55337-541-8 (bound). ISBN-13: 978-1-55337-834-1 (pbk.).
ISBN-10: 1-55337-541-6 (bound). ISBN-10: 1-55337-834-2 (pbk.)

1. Knots and splices — Juvenile literature. I. Gagnon, Céleste II. Title. III. Series.

TT751.S18 2006   j746.42'2   C2005-903650-8

Kids Can Press is a *l*𝐨𝐫𝐮𝐬™ Entertainment company

Contents

Introduction

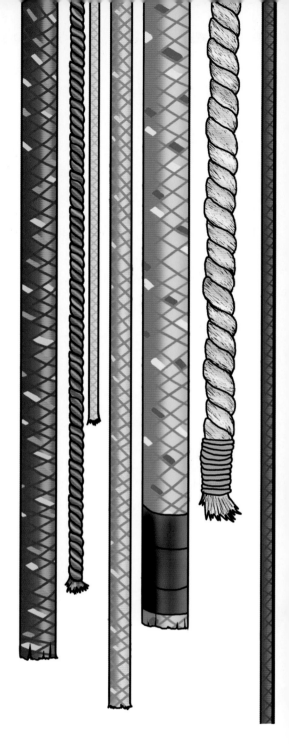

Did you know that you can already tie a
double slipped reef knot? You use it every time
you tie your shoelaces! Once you start looking,
you'll find knots everywhere: in drawstrings,
neckties, ball glove laces, garbage bags and
gift bows. Knots have been used for thousands
of years, likely first tied in plant vines and
strips of animal skins. Knotted ropes were
used in the construction of ancient pyramids
and grand stone cathedrals. Sailors perfected
countless knots during long voyages in the
days of huge sailing fleets. A sailor sometimes
even kept a new knot a secret until he could
trade his knowledge for another sailor's prized
knot. With this book you'll learn some of these
traditional knots, both simple and intricate,
then knot your way through ten terrific
projects. Create a monkey's fist fob, a new
basketball net, a rope ladder, a wooden swing
and a sample board to display all your knots.
You'll also find out what type of rope to use
and how to coil and whip it into shape. So
untangle some rope and get busy. You'll soon
have knotting all tied up!

Rope

Every project in this book is made by knotting together some type of cordage. Thick cordage is called rope, narrower cordage is called cord, line or braid and fine cordage is twine. All cordage is made by twisting or braiding together natural or synthetic fibers. Natural fibers include manila hemp, flax, jute and cotton, and some synthetic fibers are nylon, polyester and polypropylene. You'll find most of the cordage you need at hardware and building-supply stores, and you can buy colorful braid and fine cord at fabric stores. Before you buy any type of cordage, read the label for information such as the length and width of the rope, what it is made from, whether or not it is rot, mildew or abrasion resistant and how much weight it can hold. The instructions for each project in this book will tell you how much rope, cord or twine you'll need, and whether or not it should have any special qualities.

Parts of a Rope

The **working end** of the rope is the end that is being used to tie the knot.

The **standing part** and **standing end** are the parts of the rope that are not being used.

A **bight** or **open loop** refers to a bend in the rope, and it becomes a **closed loop** when the parts cross over each other.

Binding rope

When you buy rope made from synthetic fiber, you'll find that the ends are melted to prevent fraying, while the ends of natural-fiber ropes are usually taped. Once you make a new cut in your rope, the ends will come undone unless you bind them in one of the following ways.

Common whipping

1. Using a 90 cm (36 in.) piece of fine twine, make a bend in it about 10 cm (4 in.) from the end. Lay this loop along the cut rope so that it is even with the end of the rope.

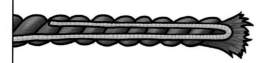

2. Starting 4 cm (1½ in.) from the end of the rope, wind the working end of the twine around the rope and both parts of the twine loop, leaving out the tail end of the twine.

3. Continue to tightly wind the twine toward the end of the rope without overlapping any of the rounds. When you have whipped about 3 cm (1¼ in.) of the rope, bring the working end through the twine loop.

4. Pull the tail end of the twine so that the loop becomes tighter and carries the working end about halfway under the whipping. Trim both ends.

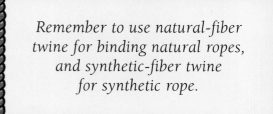

Remember to use natural-fiber twine for binding natural ropes, and synthetic-fiber twine for synthetic rope.

West country whipping

Using a 90 cm (36 in.) piece of fine twine, bring the ends together, then tie an overhand knot (page 10) about 4 cm (1½ in.) from the end of the rope. Turn the rope over and make another overhand knot on the opposite side. Keep making knots on one side and then the other until you've whipped about 3 cm (1¼ in.) toward the end of the rope. (If your whipping twine is slippery, tie double overhand knots instead.)

Finish with a reef knot (page 11) and trim the ends. Use blunt scissors or an opened paper clip to poke the cut ends under the whipping.

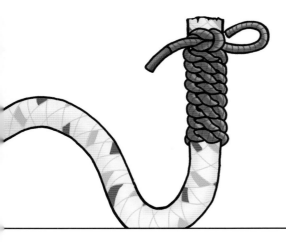

Taping

This is the easiest way to bind rope ends, but tape is only temporary and should be replaced with a knot or whipping when you are finished the project. Simply wrap the area to be cut with masking, cloth, electrical or duct tape. Cut through the center of the taped area with scissors or, for heavier rope, ask an adult to help you cut it with a sharp utility knife.

Knotting

For lightweight braid, cord and twine, you can simply tie an overhand knot, a double overhand knot or a figure-of-eight knot (page 10) near the ends. This will prevent the ends from fraying beyond the knot.

Sealing

You can dab clear nail polish on the ends of fine cordage after it has been cut. Or you can apply polish to the area of fine cordage to be cut, allow it to dry, then cut through the center of the area so both ends are done at once.

Coiling rope

The only knots you should find in your rope are the ones that you tie into it! Use this **Alpine coil** to keep each length of rope smooth, tangle-free and ready for the next project.

Hold one end of the rope in the palm of your hand, leaving a 30 cm (12 in.) tail. Bend your elbow and hold your arm straight up with your palm facing you. Wind the rope around your elbow, then between your thumb and fingers. Keep winding the rope in this way until it is all coiled.

Remove the coil from your arm and hold it in your hand. Bend back one of the ends of the rope to form a loop about 10 cm (4 in.) long along the top of the coil. Take the other end (if it is very short, unwind it from the coil by one round) and use it to wrap around the far end of the loop you just made as well as the coiled rope.

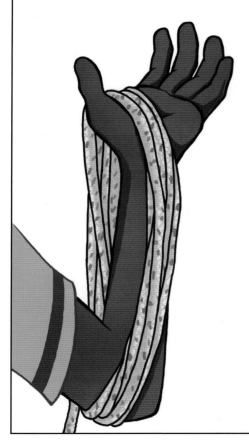

Now wind it once away from the loop so that you catch the first wind and prevent it from slipping.

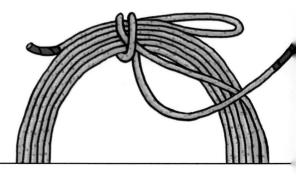

Make five or six more winds toward the loop, then tuck the working end into the loop. Pull the other end of the rope so that the loop becomes small and catches the working end.

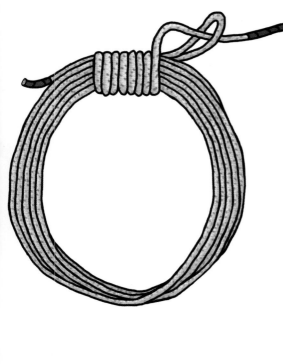

Another simple way to fasten a coil of rope is to wind it on your arm using an Alpine coil (page 8), remove it and hold it in your hand. Pick up one of the rounds other than the first or last one and use it to circle around the coil near the top. Bring it through the space you've just created below your hand. Let go of the coil of rope and hang it up by the new loop.

MEASURING ROPE

For many projects, you will need long lengths of rope or twine. Make it easier to measure them by marking a set length such as 1.5 m (5 ft.) on a table or floor and measuring the rope against it.

Knots to know

Overhand knot

Also known as a simple knot, single knot or thumb knot, you'll use this knot a lot.

Cross the working end over the standing part and bring it through the loop you just formed. Pull on the working end to tighten the knot.

Double overhand knot

This knot is the same as the overhand knot except that you bring the working end through the loop twice instead of once.

Two-strand overhand knot

This knot is tied the same way as the overhand knot but with two cords instead of one. Try to keep the cords side by side as you make the knot.

Overhand loop

Bend over one end of your cord or rope to form a loop. Tie the looped end into an overhand knot.

Figure-of-eight knot

1. Cross the working end over the standing part to form a closed loop.

2. Bring the working end around behind the standing part.

3. Bring it forward through the loop and pull it in the opposite direction from the standing end.

Ring hitch

The ring hitch is also called the lark's head, cow hitch or tag loop.

1. Double a cord and push the looped end through the ring or around the bar.

2. Open the loop and bring the cord ends through it.

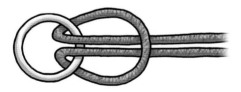

3. Pull the ends tight so the loop is snug against the ring or bar.

Reef knot

This knot is also known as a square knot.

1. Cross the right end over the left end and bring it through the loop you just made.

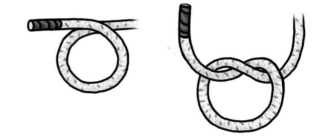

2. Now cross the new left end over the right end and through the new loop.

3. Pull the ends in opposite directions to tighten the knot. Both ends should be at the top of the knot.

Cross-knot whistle lanyard

Featuring: Chinese cross knot, reef knot, ring hitch

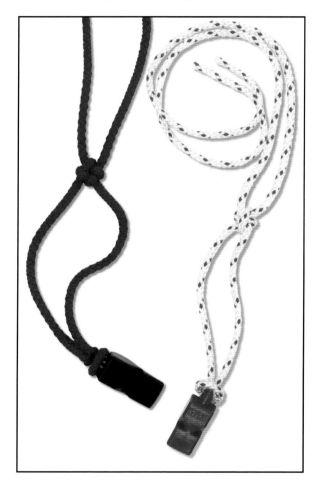

The Chinese cross knot is interesting because it looks different on the back than on the front. Instead of a whistle, you can attach keys, a compass or a pendant to your lanyard.

1 Fold the cord in half with the ends hanging over the edge of your work surface. Tape it 13 cm (5 in.) from the bent end.

2 Working just below the tape, bring the right-hand cord behind the left-hand cord and then across it so that the cord is back to the right side. It should look as if there is a half circle on the right side and, just below it, a half circle on the left side.

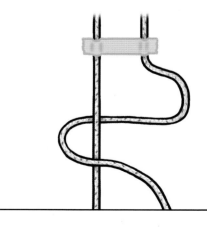

3 Take the left-hand cord and bring it up into the half circle on the right, then down behind the cord on the right. You'll now have a half circle shape at the bottom of your knotting area, too.

4 Bring the right-hand cord end behind the other one and up into the newly formed half circle.

5 Remove the tape and pull gently on each of the four cord ends. When this knot is complete, it should look like a cross on one side and a four-part square on the other side.

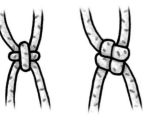

6 Attach the whistle to the lanyard with a ring hitch (page 11). If the whistle doesn't have a ring on it, attach a split-ring key ring to the lanyard with a ring hitch so that you'll be able to attach your whistle to the lanyard.

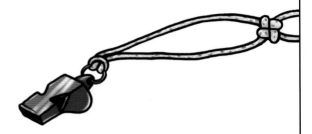

7 Tie the ends of the lanyard into a reef knot (page 11). If the lanyard is too long, cut a little off each end and bind it.

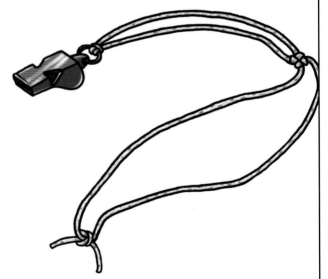

8 If you wish to fasten the lanyard to your belt loop so you can carry it in your pocket, tie the ends together with a two-strand overhand knot (page 10) instead of a reef knot. You can then fasten it to your belt loop with a ring hitch.

Monkey's fist fob

Featuring: monkey's fist knot

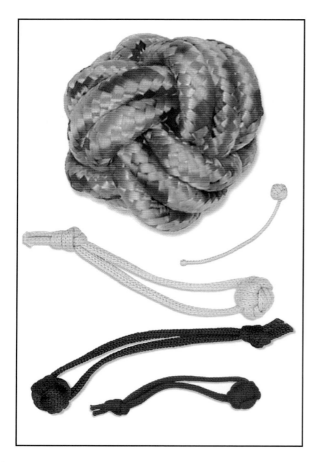

Once you get the hang of making this unique knot, you'll want one for a jacket zipper, pencil case, backpack, doorknob, key chain, belt loop, hat and even your shoes.

1 Hold up your left index and middle fingers. Hold the end of the rope against the base of your middle finger with your thumb, leaving a 25 cm (10 in.) tail. Loosely wind the rope around your two fingers three times without overlapping it.

2 Loosely wind the rope three times around the loops the other way, between your fingers.

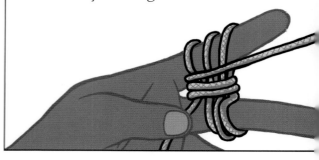

3 Slide the loops off your fingers. Wind a third set of three loops around the second set of loops, in the spaces left by your fingers. Don't overlap the loops as you wind them.

4 The secret to making a monkey's fist knot is to tighten it cord by cord into a round shape. Pull gently on one of the ends to see where it leads, then tighten that loop. Keep tightening the loop around the knot until you reach the start of the rope. You may need to do this a couple of times. Don't pull too tightly or you may end up with loops that are pulled out of place.

5 When you are pleased with the shape of your monkey's fist, there are a few ways to finish it off, depending on what you wish to do with it.

• You can trim off one of the ends very close to the knot, then dab it with nail polish. Thread the remaining end through the hole in a zipper pull and knot it in place with an overhand knot or figure-of-eight knot (page 10).

• Trim both ends to about 15 cm (6 in.). Tie them together in a two-strand overhand knot (page 10) so your knot is ready to be hung up.

• Another option is to trim off both ends, dab them with nail polish and keep the round monkey's fist for a pocket knot.

KNOT AGAIN!

• Make a tiny knot with fine twine or a gigantic knot with thick rope.

15

Square-knot guitar strap

Featuring: overhand knot, alternating square knot

These instructions use green and black cord, but choose whatever colors you like. Make sure the strap is securely fastened to your guitar before you begin to play.

1 Make a figure-of-eight knot (page 10) in the end of each cord, or dab each end with nail polish and allow them to dry.

2 Bend one of the green cords in half and make a small overhand loop (page 10) in the center. This loop will attach the strap to the knob on the guitar, so make sure it fits tightly.

3 Hook the loop onto the paper clip, then tape the paper clip to your work surface.

4 Thread one of the black cords through the right side of the overhand loop and pull until one end is 1.5 m (5 ft.) longer than the other end. Fasten it there with an overhand knot (page 10). Leave a small space and tie a two-strand overhand knot (page 10) in the black cord. Position the cords so that the long end of the black cord is on the left.

5 Fasten the other black cord the same way except position it on the left of the knot in the green cord. Leave a small space and tie a two-strand overhand knot in this black cord, too, making sure the long cord end is on the right.

6 Thread a green cord into the new loop in the black cord on the left-hand side. Pull the green cord until the ends are even, then position the green cords between the black cords.

7 Bring the left-hand cord across the center cords and behind the right-hand cord. This forms a half circle on the left side.

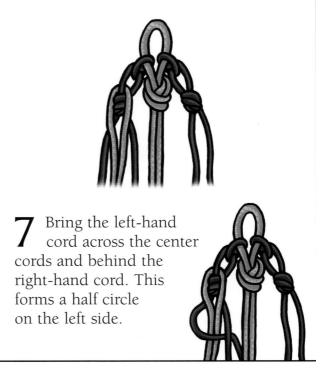

Instructions continue on the next page ☞

8 Bring the right-hand cord behind the center cords and pull it toward you through the half circle on the left.

9 Gently pull both cords so that the knot moves up the center cords, then pull firmly on the cords so the half knot is tight.

10 Bring the right-hand cord across the center cords and behind the left-hand cord. This forms a half circle on the right side.

11 Bring the left-hand cord behind the center cords and pull it toward you through the half circle on the right. Gently pull both cords so that the knot moves up the center cords to the half knot, then pull firmly on the cords so the knot is tight. This completes a square knot.

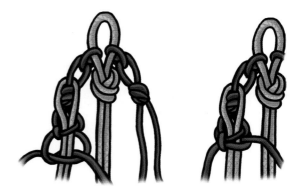

12 Repeat steps 6 to 11 on the right-hand side.

13 Leave a small space, then make a square knot around the two green cords in the center by using the longer black cord from the left-hand knot and the longer black cord from the right-hand knot.

14 Leave a small space and make another square knot on the right side, left side and in the center. Keep knotting in this alternating square knot pattern. (If you like, you can roll up the extra lengths of cord and fasten them with rubber bands.) Depending on the size and style of your guitar, the strap should be 120 cm to 150 cm (48 in. to 60 in.) long.

15 To finish the strap, tie a square knot on each side using three center cords. Tie all the ends in a large overhand knot. You may need to trim off the leftover cords (see step 1 to bind the ends).

16 To attach the strap to your guitar, hook the green loop over the small knob on one end of the guitar, then place it around your neck. If the guitar has another knob near the neck, hook the strap onto it through one of the square-knot holes. If it doesn't have another knob, tie the strap to the peg head (near the tuning keys) with a small piece of cord.

Overhand-knot bottle holder

Featuring: ring hitch, square knot, two-strand overhand knot

You can sling this handy holder over your shoulder or fasten it to your backpack with a carabiner, a handy clip with a spring-loaded latch.

1 Bend one cord in half and attach it to the ring with a ring hitch (page 11). Attach the other seven cords the same way. Tighten them by pulling on each of the cord ends.

2 Take the right-hand cord from one of the pairs of cords and put it with the left-hand cord from the pair beside it. Grip the other cords between your knees as you tie these two cords into a two-strand overhand knot (page 10) about 2 cm (3/4 in.) from the ring.

3 Continue around the ring, knotting each cord with a cord from the pair beside it. You should now have a row of ring hitches and a row of overhand knots.

4 Leave a 2 cm (3/4 in.) space and make another row of overhand knots centered between the first row of overhand knots. This will start a diamond pattern.

5 Tie another row of overhand knots to continue the diamond pattern.

6 Place the water bottle in the base of the holder and fasten it with the rubber band. Keep knotting until you have seven or eight rows of overhand knots.

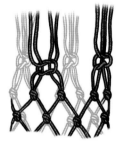

7 For the handles, take two pairs of side-by-side cords and make a square knot (steps 7 to 11, pages 17 to 18). Make square knots in the other three sets of cords, too.

8 For the next set of square knots, leave a 2 cm (3/4 in.) space and then switch the cords so that you are using the tying cords in the center and the center cords for tying. Make at least five more sets of square knots, switching the tying and center cords each time.

9 When the handles are long enough (or you are running out of cord), gather all sixteen cords together and tie them in an overhand knot. Trim the ends and let them fray.

Wound-rope ladder

Featuring: overhand loop

It's amazing to think that you can make a ladder with nothing but a few knots in a length of rope. The measurements given will make a ladder with four or five rungs. Use more rope for a longer ladder.

1 Bend the rope in half. Make an overhand knot (page 10), leaving a 15 cm (6 in.) loop. Hang the loop on a strong hook, nail or doorknob.

2 Starting at the top, run each side of the rope through your hands to smooth it out. Separate the two lines and fasten each into a loose bundle with a rubber band.

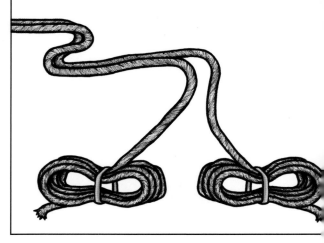

3 Make a bend in the left-hand rope, 30 cm (12 in.) from the overhand knot. Bring the rope behind and around the right-hand rope, back to the left side and then back to the right side. This is the start of a rung — it should be about 20 cm (8 in.) across.

4 Wind the bundled right-hand rope under, then around, the three lines of rope that form the rung. Make about 15 rounds, winding them very tightly side by side.

5 When you get to the left side, undo the bundle and feed the entire length of the rope through the loop there. Bundle the rope again.

6 Adjust the rung so that both sides are an even distance from the top. Tug firmly on both ropes to make the rung tight.

Instructions continue on the next page ☞

7 Leave a 25 cm (10 in.) space, then make another rung by repeating steps 3 to 6. Make two or three more rungs the same way. As your ladder gets longer, hook one of the rungs onto two hooks or nails or on double closet doorknobs.

9 To help prevent your ladder from spiraling as you climb it, try fastening it to a tree limb with a ring hitch (page 11), or at step 8, leave more rope on each end and hang it upside down using swing hitches (steps 6 to 9, pages 26 to 27).

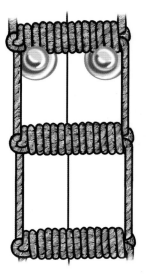

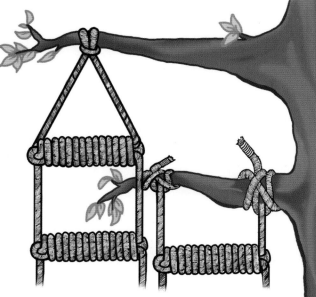

8 Leaving at least 60 cm (24 in.) (see step 9), make a figure-of-eight knot (page 10) at the end of each rope. Trim any leftover rope and whip the ends (page 6).

10 As you climb the ladder, have someone hold the rope at the bottom, or use sturdy pegs to fasten the ends of the rope in place.

Swing-hitch rope swing

Featuring: swing hitch

It's easy to make a good old-fashioned wooden swing. Most lumber stores will cut a piece of wood the right size for you.

1 Wearing safety glasses, have an adult help you drill a 2.5 cm (1 in.) hole centered 5 cm (2 in.) from each side. (If you are using an electric hand drill, it's best to place the board on a larger piece of wood on the floor. Kneel on the end of the swing seat opposite the end you are drilling.)

2 Sand the seat so no one will get a splinter from it. Paint or stain the seat if you like, following the manufacturer's instructions. Let it dry.

Instructions continue on the next page ☞

3 Check the label (or check with the store staff) to make sure that the rope you buy is strong enough to support someone on the swing. To figure out how much rope you'll need, measure the distance from the tree limb or bar to where you'd like the swing to hang. Double the length and add about 2.5 m (8 ft.). Whip the ends of the rope (page 6).

4 Thread one end of the rope through one of the holes, across the bottom of the seat and up through the other hole.

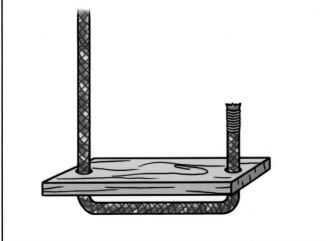

5 Choose a strong, thick tree limb or swing-set bar to hang up your swing. Have someone hold the seat as you tie the knots.

6 The working end should be at least 60 cm to 90 cm (24 in. to 36 in.) long. Hold the working end of the rope behind the limb or bar, wind it forward around the limb and back up behind it, slanting the rope to the upper left.

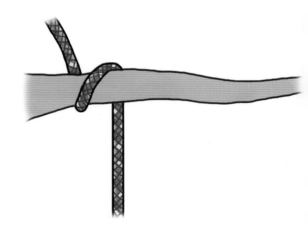

7 Bring the working end forward, slanting it down to the right. Tuck it under the loop you made on the limb in step 6. This makes an **X** shape.

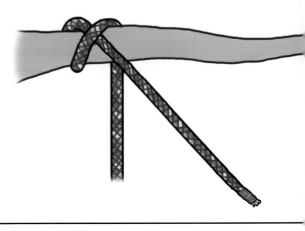

8 Wind the working end up behind the limb, then bring it forward and tuck the end under the new loop you just made.

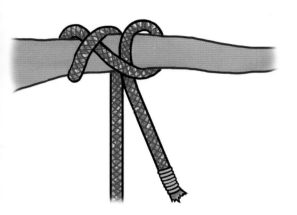

9 Bring the working end around behind the standing part of the rope (the hanging part), then tuck it straight up under the **X** shape you made in step 7. Tighten the knot and push the parts together.

10 Tie the other rope end onto the limb or bar the same way.

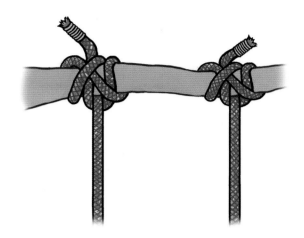

11 You can adjust the height of the swing by tying an overhand loop into the rope under the seat (or re-tying one of the swing hitches). Check the condition of the rope and limb or bar periodically to make sure they're still strong and safe.

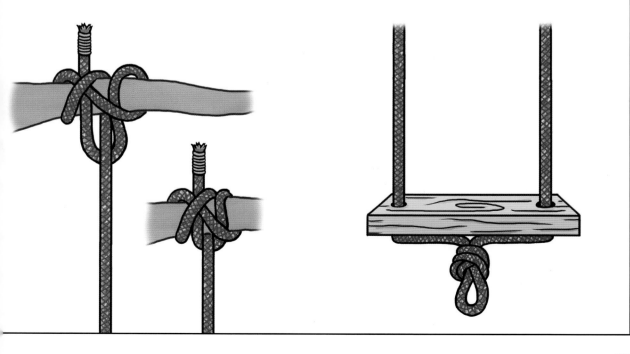

Eight-strand braided dog leash

Featuring: ring hitch, eight-strand braid, square knot

These instructions use yellow and blue twine, but you can use any colors you like. Choose thin, but very strong, nylon cord or twine. Be sure to regularly check that the leash is in good shape before you clip it onto your dog's collar.

1 Tape the swivel-bolt snap to your work surface.

2 Fold one of the blue cords in half and attach it to the swivel-bolt snap using a ring hitch (page 11). Attach the other three cords the same way.

3 You should now have four lengths of blue twine on the left and four shorter lengths of yellow twine on the right. Wind one of the cord ends around a couple of your fingers. Leave about 30 cm (12 in.) of the cord unbundled, then fasten the bundle with a rubber band. Bundle the other seven cords the same way.

4 Bring the blue cord on the far left behind five of the cords closest to it and up through the middle of the four yellow cords. Now pass it back to the left across two yellow cords to the blue side. This time it will be the blue cord closest to the yellow cords.

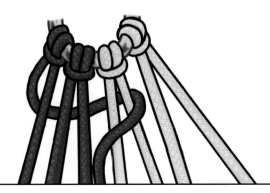

5 Bring the yellow cord on the far right behind five of the cords closest to it and up through the middle of the four blue cords. Now pass it back to the right across two blue cords to the yellow side. This time it will be the yellow cord closest to the blue cords.

6 Keep the cords separated by pulling the blue cords to the left side and the yellow cords to the right side.

Instructions continue on the next page ☞

7 Repeat steps 5 and 6. After you've braided about 2.5 cm (1 in.), tighten the braided area by pulling firmly on each individual cord. The braid will take on a square shape.

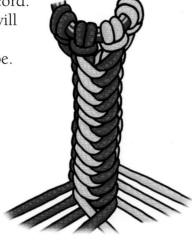

9 When you have about 85 cm (33 in.) of eight-strand braid, remove the rubber band from each bundle. Rearrange the cords so that the four yellow cords are in the center and two blue ones are on each side. You'll now begin knotting the handle.

8 Keep braiding, always keeping it tight. Gently pull out cord from the bundles as you need it. If you have to stop braiding, use tape or paper clips to hold the cords in place until you are ready to braid again. As the leash gets longer, you may wish to remove the tape from the bolt snap and re-tape the leash farther down the braiding.

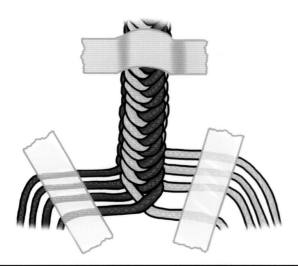

10 See steps 7 to 11 on pages 17 to 18 for how to make a square knot. The only difference is that you'll be knotting with two cords on the left, two on the right and four in the center. Tie the knots tightly, but leave a bit of space between each knot so that you can see the yellow cords, too.

11 Make square knots until the handle is about 30 cm (12 in.) long. Remove the tape from the swivel snap and turn the leash around. Fold over the square-knotted area and use the twist tie to hold the shape of a handle. Tape down the handle so that the knotted area is on top and the unknotted cords are underneath.

13 Make another square knot, this time using the blue cords for tying and the yellow cords and braid in the center. Remove the twist tie.

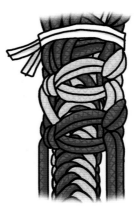

12 Separate the four yellow cords and use them to tie a square knot with the blue cords and braid in the center. Make sure the knots are tied tightly.

14 Hold the eight cords together and choose the two longest ones. Using west country whipping (page 7), bind the remaining cords to the braided area for a length of about 5 cm (2 in.).

15 Trim all the ends short.

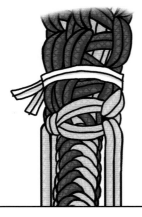

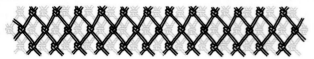

Netting-knot basketball net

Featuring: netting knot and two-strand overhand knot

Is your basketball net ripped or missing? Here's how to make one yourself. Use cord that is rot and mildew resistant and not too stiff. You'll be using a sheet-bend knot, but when it is used in net-making, it is called a netting knot or a mesh knot.

1 Shape the hanger into a circle. Place the hook of the hanger on the edge of a table and stack some heavy books on it.

2 Make a small cut on one end of the narrow strip of cardboard and squeeze one end of the cord into it. Wind the cord neatly around the cardboard. When you are finished, you'll have a few layers of cord.

3 Place the cord on the floor below the hanger. From within the hanger, loop the end of the cord over the edge. Leave a 100 cm (40 in.) tail. Fasten the cord to the hanger with a clothespin.

6 One at a time, remove the loops from the cardboard and fasten each one to the hanger with a clothespin. Keeping the loops in order, slide the clothespins around the hanger so that the loops are evenly spaced.

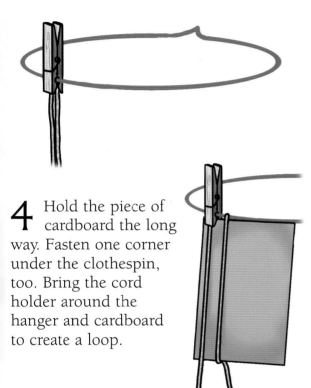

4 Hold the piece of cardboard the long way. Fasten one corner under the clothespin, too. Bring the cord holder around the hanger and cardboard to create a loop.

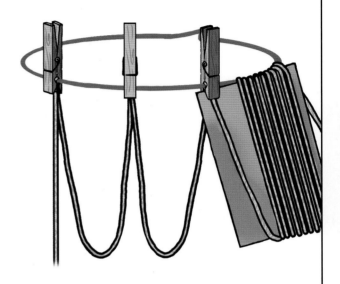

7 Carefully remove each clothespin and fasten the loops in place with masking tape.

5 Make 10 more loops the same way. Keep the loops side by side without overlapping them.

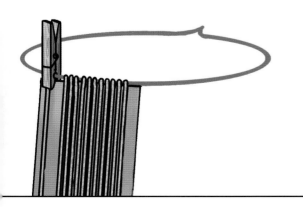

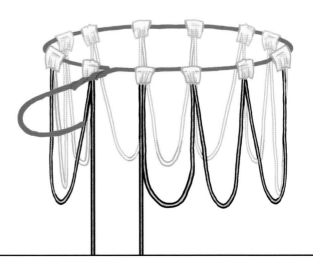

Instructions continue on the next page ☞

8 The tail end of the cord and the working cord should now be close together, one on each side of the hook. Tie them together with a two-strand overhand knot (page 10) so that this loop is the same length as the ones beside it. (It may be awkward to tie because you will have to feed through the bundle of cord along with the tail end.)

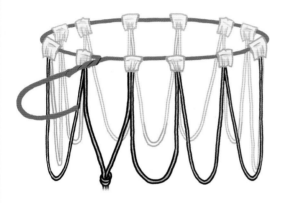

9 Unwind some of the cord and, from behind, bring the cord holder forward through the loop.

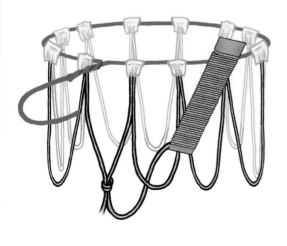

10 With your left hand, pull the cord a little to the left of the loop creating a half-circle shape.

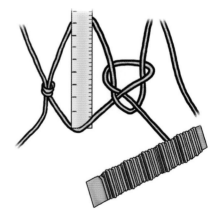

11 Bring the cord holder around behind the loop and through the half circle you just made. Pull the cord downward to the right. Before you tighten the knot, make sure that the distance from the hanger to the new loop is about 23 cm (9 in.). Tighten the netting knot by first pulling on the two lower cords, then the other two cords.

12 Continue knotting around the hanger, changing the position of the hanger as you go. If your cord becomes twisted, turn the cord holder a couple of times in the opposite direction.

13 When you reach the tail end, instead of making a netting knot, join the working cord to the tail with a two-strand overhand knot. The new loop should be the same length as the others in the row.

15 Keep knotting for about eight rows. When you've reached the tail end again, join the working cord to the tail end with a two-strand overhand knot. Trim the ends short and dab them with nail polish.

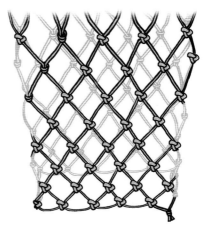

14 For the next row, you'll be knotting onto the center of the loops you just made. To keep the loops even, use the cardboard from steps 4 to 6 the short way as a guide. It should fit between the new loop and the knot directly above it.

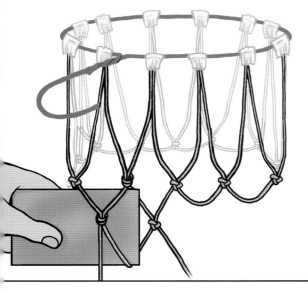

16 Remove the masking tape and open the hanger by carefully untwisting the hook. Slide the net off and ask an adult to help you hang it up. If you're missing some of the net holders, tie that part of the net onto the basketball hoop with pieces of cord.

Netting-knot sports bag

Featuring: netting knot and two-strand overhand knot

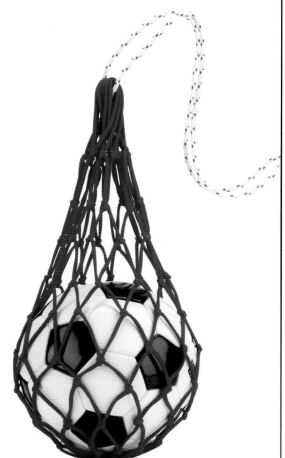

This open-mesh bag is perfect for holding a basketball, football, soccer ball, towel and bathing suit or whatever else you need to carry to your game or practice.

1 Follow steps 1 to 4 on pages 32 to 33, except at step 4, hold the piece of cardboard the short way so you end up with smaller loops.

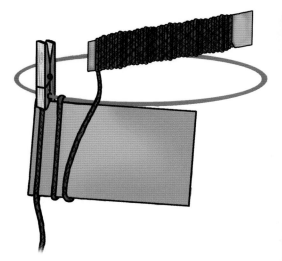

2 Continue with steps 5 to 13 on pages 33 to 35, except in steps 11 to 13 the distance from the hanger to each new loop in the first row should be 13 cm (5 in.).

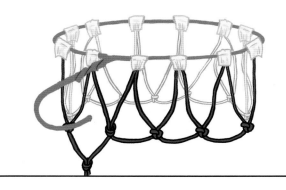

3 Follow steps 14 and 15. If you like, you can knot more than eight rows for a longer bag.

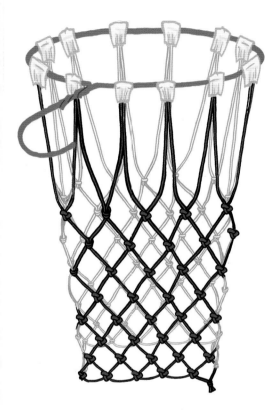

4 After you've made the bag the length you'd like, gather the bottom loops onto your finger, then onto the key ring. It's helpful to hold the key ring open with a clothespin or ruler.

5 Remove the masking tape and open the hanger carefully by untwisting the hook. Slide the bag off. Weave a leftover 120 cm (48 in.) piece of cord (or a thicker piece of cord) through the top loops. Fasten the ends with a two-strand overhand knot (page 10).

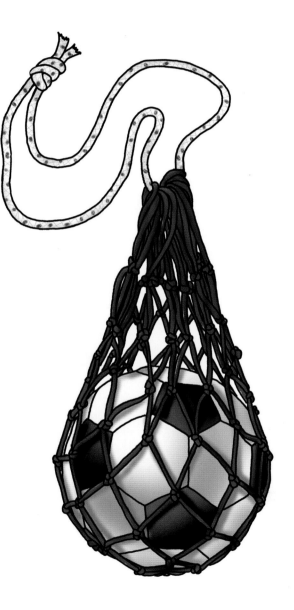

Knots-to-know sample board

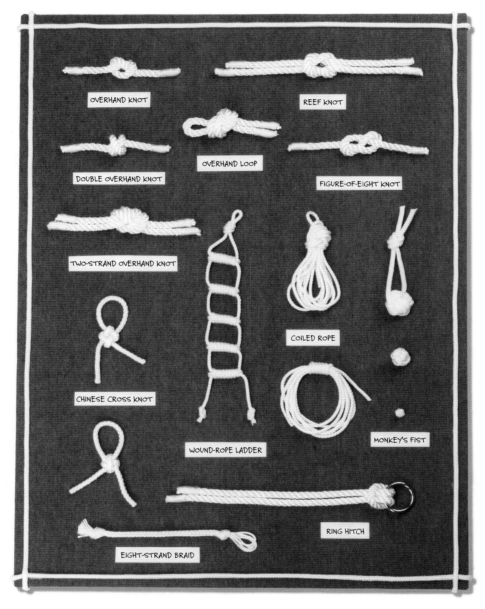

OVERHAND KNOT

REEF KNOT

DOUBLE OVERHAND KNOT

OVERHAND LOOP

FIGURE-OF-EIGHT KNOT

TWO-STRAND OVERHAND KNOT

COILED ROPE

CHINESE CROSS KNOT

WOUND-ROPE LADDER

MONKEY'S FIST

RING HITCH

EIGHT-STRAND BRAID

Here's a great way to display some of the interesting knots
you've learned. You can make the sample board whatever size you like.
If you want to include all the knots in this book, you will need a
board about 45 cm x 60 cm (18 in. x 24 in.).

- a heavy canvas board or a piece of plywood
- fabric slightly larger than your board or acrylic craft paint and a paintbrush (optional)
- small nails and a hammer or a hot glue gun (ask an adult to help you)
- leftover pieces of cordage
- scissors
- heavy paper or cardstock and markers, or a computer and printer
- a frame without glass (optional)

1 You can leave your sample board unfinished or cover it with fabric or paint. If you use fabric, smooth it over the front of the board. Flip the board over and use hot glue to attach the edges of the fabric to the back of the board.

2 Since you're using lots of short pieces of cordage, bind the ends (page 6) using different methods. Make the same knot in different sizes and colors of cordage.

Here are some ideas:

- When you tie small knots such as the overhand (page 10) or figure-of-eight (page 10), use thick cord or rope so that it is easy to see how the knot is made.

- Tie the swing hitch (page 27) around a piece of dowel or a trimmed branch.

- Tie the ring hitch (page 11) onto a small ring.

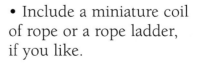

- Include a miniature coil of rope or a rope ladder, if you like.

Instructions continue on the next page ☞

3 Decide how you'd like to arrange the samples on your board. Do you want the knots in rows or a circle? You could have some around the edges of the board with your favorite knots in the center.

4 To attach the samples to your board, you can either hammer small nails into the board and hang up the samples, or use hot glue.

5 Create labels for your knots by hand or using a computer. Glue them under the samples on the board.

6 Be sure to sign your name and the date on the front or back of the board with paint or a permanent marker.

7 When you're finished, you may wish to frame your sample board or have it done professionally in a box frame with glass.

KNOT AGAIN!

Are there knots that you'd like to practice? If so, get an adult to help you drill small holes into the board. Thread rope or cord through the holes. This works especially well for a knot such as the reef knot.